Manners, Please!

Poems and Activities That Teach Responsible Behavior

by Greta Barclay Lipson, Ed.D.
illustrated by Teresa Mathis

Teaching & Learning Company
1204 Buchanan St., P.O. Box 10
Carthage, IL 62321

Cover by Teresa Mathis

Copyright © 1995, Teaching & Learning Company

ISBN No. 1-57310-014-5

Printing No. 987

Teaching & Learning Company
1204 Buchanan St., P.O. Box 10
Carthage, IL 62321

This book belongs to

_____

Table of Contents

Don't Be Uncouth

Please and Thank You

Elmore Interrupts Us

Achoo-Gesundheit

Never, Ever, Pick Your Nose!

Let's Hear You Say, "Hello!"

TLC10014 Copyright © Teaching & Learning Company, Carthage, IL 62321

Dear Teacher or Parent,

The most important thing about manners is that they offer us safety—a kind of behavioral map which helps us in our expectations of one another. Social rules offer us protection and security without having to improvise on our own. Just as the law codifies society's beliefs, so do good manners express the refinement and the humanity of a society in which we respect ourselves and all others with equal concern. Manners help us get along with one another.

The etiquette cognoscenti may not agree, but it is this author's belief that protocol (the correct form) is much less important than a youngster's social awareness and good intentions. I come to this view as one of my maternal grandmother's 21 grandchildren. For her, the touchstone of acceptable behavior was always, "was the kid's heart in the right place?" She was not a hard liner but was concerned with larger issues than elbows on the table. Hers was a softer approach, moored to the reality of a house spilling over with kids, adults and dogs. It is my grandmother's pragmatic approach to which I heartily subscribe.

Therefore it is the purpose and direction of this book of manners to promote sensitivity and civilized behavior in children. In answer to the question: Can schools teach character and integrity? Our answer must be a resounding, Yes! But it is, emphatically, the societal obligation of all of us to improve the quality of our children's lives. This is not the sole domain of the school. The critical foundation is established at home by a caring family—and in all places where adults are expected to behave according to an accepted code of civility.

The old axiom cautions us that "You can't judge a book by its cover." But if we are honest, we must admit that, of course, we do it all the time. We make judgements of people which are influenced by their demeanor and appearance. Our standards are based upon the way people act, speak, dress and conduct themselves in their interaction with family and countless others in the course of a day.

A smile, a greeting, a helping hand, a pleasant encounter in the workplace, a thoughtful gesture in the supermarket, a thank-you wave from a motorist, all of these actions serve to give our days gentility and harmony. This social cordiality affects one's spirit and gives us a measure of internal calm and warmth. Good manners make life tolerable for all of us—young and old alike.

It is clearly in our power to make daily living smoother, and more comfortable by internalizing and practicing good manners consistently in all of our contacts. These refinements in our attitudes and consideration of others affects the quality of our lives significantly. And that makes us feel worthy and good about ourselves, as well! What we give to others is returned to us in kind.

Let us commit ourselves to the task and proceed to educate the humanity of our children. It is important to remember that the young learn by observing, and it is we adults who model for them. As the dutiful mother said to her obstreperous toddler, "Make nice, baby!"—And so, the social awareness begins.

This is a true-to-life book.

Sincerely,

Greta

Greta Barclay Lipson, Ed.D.

Foreword

by Ms. Ro Schilke, Principal
Warren G. Harding Elementary School
Ferndale, Michigan

One need only spend minutes walking around school–in the lunchroom, the playground during recess, in hallways and class-rooms–to appreciate the need for Dr. Greta Lipson's valuable book, *Manners, Please!*

Just as gears need grease to run quietly, and machines need oil to be efficient, children need to have practice in acceptable social behaviors. With this advantage they are better able to interact with others and function more comfortably in our very complicated society.

Your students will recognize themselves and others in this collection of daily foibles as Dr. Lipson helps us accept our imperfections and inspires us to do better! This strategy is an enormous help in prac-ticing social skills as we come to recognize the need to improve manners on a daily basis.

As an elementary school principal, and a teacher through the grades, I have learned never to ask the fatal question: "Is that the sort of thing you do at home?" Often it is *indeed* the sort of thing students do at home!

Teachers will chuckle and shake their heads in agreement and appreciation to have a guide, such as this, to be used in the class-room. It is guaranteed to help pave the way!

Laughter, the rhythm of poetry, (and serious thought) is the key to these successful lessons!

How to Use This Book

Given the range of skills among students–process this material through the grid of your own teaching experience and the needs of your pupils on their level. You (above all) know how far they can reach for success. As always, it is your insightful call.

- Define *manners* as, "shared, socially appropriate behavior."
- Discuss the reasons for manners and polite behavior in a social context.
- Explain the format of this book which includes an introductory poem and picture for a variety of manners, followed by activities for discussion, writing and creative expression.
- Capitalize on both positive and negative examples from real life.
- Allow for humor and good-natured laughter.
- Personalize the theme with open discussion and experience.
- Support individuality! Encourage your students to participate with their own opinions.
- Help students analyze the reasons for some prescribed behavior which they may not understand.
- Participate with your students by recounting your own experiences.
- Stimulate lively responses by reading the poems aloud and helping the children participate orally.
- Use suggested activities as a springboard and improvise others of choice which are relative to each subject.
- Involve the children in dramatic play or recitation, when possible, to demonstrate the poems and/or activities.

Some specific suggestions are on the folllowing pages.

Suggestions

1. Highlight a chapter a week on the bulletin board. Use an opaque projector to copy the poem and its illustration for the week. Use black marker on white butcher paper. Have the children color the picture with colored markers or any vivid medium of choice.

2. Initiate student efforts to produce personal manners booklets. Students may use reproduced pages from this book, enhanced by their own written commentary, observations and experience. Use a snapshot of each child as the basis for a book cover design.

3. Conduct voluntary role play situations to emphasize manners issues. In cameo performances, allow for interpretations and the mixing of adult and children's roles and points of view.

4. Try choral speaking with the poems, organizing groups to take specific parts. Work through the possibilities of the rhythm of the poetry using voice, pitch and dramatic expression. Invite suggestions from the class. Pass out copies of the poems to the students for practice sessions. Rehearsal can be as much fun as the finished performance, since this is school and not Broadway! A venturesome music teacher may be invited to participate in this enterprise.

5. Use the coloring page activity to reinforce the concepts in the poem. Coloring pages can be sent home for children to discuss with their families, displayed on the classroom bulletin board or collected in students' portfolios. An added feature on each coloring page is finding the hidden character, Etta Kett.

6. Confer the Good Manners Award (see page 82) once a week to *one* student with formality and ceremony. The place holder for the principal's signature on the award confers special status to the certificate.

7. Capitalize on the letters of inquiry sent to Ms. Etta Kett (see page 84) deposited in the classroom mailbox, with questions regarding manners. Search for students' answers and opinions through illuminating discussion.

8. Encourage each child to offer the Praise Page (see page 83) to a friend, neighbor, classmate or family member who will attest to the courtesy of the student and will write something positive in support of that student.

9. Set aside a brief period of time for a session called, "Applause! Applause!" to last for as many weeks as you choose. This sequence allows for an individual to announce to the class something mannerly, good-hearted or courteous done by the presenter, for example, "I took out the garbage and my mother didn't even ask me to do it." This is followed by enthusiastic applause from the listeners.

10. Prepare the class for an interview experience in which each student asks an adult at home a prepared and incisive question about the importance of good manners. The answers are to be written by the student and returned to class to be shared by anyone who volunteers to read his responses.

11. Organize a Hats Off Day for your classroom, for a grade level assembly or for a schoolwide affair. Explain the metaphor "hats off" as being an expression which acknowledges a person's fine qualities. In this case it may be in recognition of the civility, courtesy and good manners of a particular person or entire class which has improved the school environment. Each student may bring in a wildly decorated hat to wear for the morning or afternoon of this special tribute.

For the Students

Are manners important? Yes, indeed they are. If you lived in a cave all by yourself and ate with your fingers and grunted and scratched yourself all day long and only washed once in a while and had no friends or family then–manners wouldn't matter!

But you don't live in a cave! You are a civilized human being! You have a family; you go to school; you live in a neighborhood with other children and adults. You want to love and be loved as you share your world with others, all the hours of the day.

When people live and work together there are rules to be followed which make life smooth and happy! The rules of behavior are called GOOD MANNERS, and it is easy to learn what to do if you remember one important thing: Treat other people kindly and with consideration–just exactly the way you want to be treated yourself.

Good manners make you a lovable, considerate person! Others will enjoy being around you. When you learn about the right way to act, you can then teach your brothers or your sisters (or even your dog), and pretty soon everybody will try just a little harder to make the world a kinder, more courteous and gentler place!

Here is a secret: Can you believe that sometimes children have better manners than adults? How can that be? (Nobody taught these grownups in school or at home the importance of good manners!)

Don't Be Uncouth

Remember: It is very pleasant to be around a person with good manners !

I wouldn't lie
About the truth!
You won't be liked
If you're uncouth.*

So learn to be nice
Clean up your act!
You'll be loved by more people
And that's a fact!

Smooth out your style
From toes to chin
Work on your attitude
From outside in.

Say, "Please and thanks."
Say, "Howdy do."
Ask, "How are things?"
Say, "Welcome," too!

Practice your manners
Be polite
You'll win much praise
'Cause you do things right!

G.B. Lipson

*Uncouth is defined as "crude or unrefined." Couth means "refined."

Coloring Page

It's nice to be nice!

Here is Etta Kett. Can you find her hiding on this page?

2

Don't Be Uncouth

Student Activities

• In these opening activities the students will start their own construction paper *Book of Manners* which will represent a cumulative record of each of the twenty manners under discussion. The printed forms, student art and any written work of choice may be added to the book.

• The students should be encouraged to bring in snapshots of themselves to put on the cover of their books for a personalized touch. The teacher may elect to set aside a picture-taking day to take uniform snapshots of each child. Creativity is the rule of the day for the cover design.

• Attend to the Praise Page in the back of this book. On this page a teacher, parent or a classmate may write a positive statement of praise which is a comment on the good manners of the student-author. Any other original idea pages may be used for enhancement as well, such as the "Today I learned"; the manners award or advice from Ms. Etta Kett.

• Duplicate the picture to color and cut out as a paper figure. This may be pasted in the students' manners books. A second figure may be made into a mobile by punching a hole in the top and forcing a string through the hole. In this way "Uncouth" can swing from a hanger as a class mobile and as an introduction to the manners unit of studies.

Don't Be Uncouth

Writing Activities

Name: _____

> Write a short story about an uncouth person.
> Here is a starter sentence that will lead you into your make-believe tale.

You wouldn't believe what happened when I was invited to a birthday party

_____

_____

_____

_____

_____

Today I learned _____

_____

_____

_____

_____

Please and Thank You

Remember: This is a nice way to ask for something and to express your gratitude.

"Please and thank you"
Is a perfect combination.
Everyone likes the sound of it
For your information.

When you say "Please and thank you,"
Folks like the way you act.
It opens up their hearts and minds
And that's a manners fact!

So please say "Please and thank you";
It has a lovely ring.
Remember–use that winning phrase
When you ask for anything!

G.B. Lipson

Say "Please" and "Thank You"!

Here is Etta Kett. Can you find her hiding on this page?

Please and Thank You
Student Activities

- The author, Sesyle Joslin and the artist, Maurice Sendak, wrote a book entitled *What Do You Say, Dear?* He set the scene in a silly way so that the reader would have fun with a courteous response. You can do the same by using your imagination. For example: Wilma Worm invited you to dinner. She asked if you would like a hot bowl of mud soup. You said, . . . (No thank you). Dottie Dribble was eating a luscious cup of cream custard and you said, . . . (May I please have a taste?). Now you try making up these little stories.

- Do remember, *always*, to say "thank you" for a special gesture from a friend or relative when they are kind to you. Think of individuals who have done kind things for you all through the week. Make a list of these people who deserve a thank-you! (Example: a friend, teacher's aide, crossing guard, baby-sitter, grandparent, librarian, school secretary, custodian, postal carrier, sales clerk, neighbor, etc.)

- Select an individual from the list above and write a thank-you note to that person. Decorate the note to make it look like special personalized stationery. Address the envelope with the name, address, city and zip code, as if you were going to mail it. Include your return address.

- Look up the word *ingrate* in the dictionary. What does it mean? Why does that word come to mind at this time?

- If you ask for something and don't use "Please and thank you," it sounds like a command: "Give me that pencil!" "Take this away!" "Get my book!" Nobody wants to be ordered to do something, so instead we make a polite request for things. With two volunteer actors in front of the class, demonstrate the right and wrong way to ask for things.

Please and Thank You

Writing Activities

Name: _____

> Write a short story about the phrase "Please and Thank You."
> Here is a starter sentence that will lead you into your make believe tale.

Prunella rushed into the ice cream store and said, "I'll have a chocolate sundae, extra everything with two spoons and hurry up!" The clerk said, _____

_____

_____

_____

_____

_____

Today I learned _____

_____

_____

_____

_____

_____

8

Elmore Interrupts Us

Remember: Respect each person's right to speak and be heard.

When we see Elmore coming
We would like to run away
'Cause Elmore doesn't wait his turn
With things he has to say!

He interrupts and butts right in
He stops us in our tracks
He talks and talks a wild streak
He yaks and yaks and yaks!

Now here's a tip for Elmore
It's something he should say
Like, "Pardon or excuse me"
I'm in a rush today!

There's a better hint for Elmore
That won't make stomachs churn
He should talk when others finish
And try to wait his turn!

Cool it, Elmore!

G.B. Lipson

Don't interrupt!
Say, "Excuse me, please!"

Here is Etta Kett. Can you find her hiding on this page?

Elmore Interrupts Us
Student Activities

- Why do people get upset when they are interrupted? (Answer: They may forget what they were saying; it makes it seem as if what they are saying is not important; everyone wants to express a complete opinion or a thought; it is very rude).

- Under what circumstances would it be excusable to interrupt someone's conversation? (Answer: An emergency or urgent business which can't wait!)

- Have a make-believe situation in which you must interrupt two people who are having a conversation. Demonstrate to the class how you would manage to break into the conversation, courteously. Don't forget to give a reason for what you are doing. Start with, "Excuse me . . . ."

- Elmore does other things to interrupt, like pulling on the teacher's sweater all day long, to get her attention! Draw a picture of the teacher's poor stretched-out sweater at the end of the day!

- Sometimes people interrupt without thinking because they are bursting to talk. Can you remember a time when you were so anxious to talk that you could not keep quiet? What was it that you had to say so urgently?

- Pretend that three classmates form a committee to plan a menu for a Saturday party. The main course choices seem to be hot dogs, spaghetti or pizza. The problem is that they keep interrupting and they are not listening to each other! Write out a plan to use that would stop the interruptions and help the group make a decision.

Elmore Interrupts Us

Writing Activities

Name: _____

Write a short story about interrupting others.
Here is a starter sentence that will lead you into your make-believe tale.

Mayor Birdwhistle was making a speech in the park when Little Willie _____

_____

_____

_____

_____

_____

_____

Today I learned _____

_____

_____

_____

_____

_____

_____

Achoo-Gesundheit*

Remember: Practice proper hygiene and good manners for health.

Your sneeze exploded in the class
My teacher caught the flu!
The cold spread all around the room
We didn't know what to do!

We coughed and blew our noses
This story's sad but true.
A virus caused our sniffles
And we caught it all from you!

Our throats are sore and scratchy
It's spreading through the school
So cover up a cough or sneeze–

ACHOO! ACHOO! ACHOO!

G.B. Lipson

* Gesundheit: A German blessing following a
sneeze which means, "To your good health."

Cover a sneeze, if you please!

Here is ![Etta Kett icon] Etta Kett. Can you find her hiding on this page?

Achoo-Gesundheit
Student Activities

- Of course we all know that we should cover our mouths when we sneeze or cough, because nobody wants to be sprayed in the face! Most importantly, we try to do the best we can to prevent everyone around us from becoming infected with our cold. As a good reminder to others, make an art project to demonstrate the right thing to do when you cough or sneeze. On construction paper draw a large face. Include hair, ears, eyes, brows, nose and mouth. Next, trace a picture of your hand. Paste a real tissue (Kleenex®) over the mouth of your drawing. Glue or staple the cutout hand over it! At the bottom of the picture you may want to write:

   Cover your mouth when you say, Achoo!
   Or I will catch your bad cold, too!

- Doctors advise us that when we have a cold we must always be careful to wash our hands many times through the day because the infection is carried by our hands. If you are so sick that you must stay at home, what is your favorite activity to keep busy and interested? Describe your favorite comfort food or drink which you think helps you feel better. Is it a steamy bowl of chicken soup with rice? Is it a cup of hot citrus drink with honey? Or is it an old-fashioned cup of hot chocolate with a big marshmallow floating on the surface?

- If you could see a cold virus under a microscope, what do you think it would look like? Draw this dangerous nasty critter from your imagination! Give it a catchy medical name such as Vinny the Virus or The Cold Critter.

Achoo-Gesundheit

Writing Activities

Name: _____

> Write a short story about sneezing.
> Here is a starter sentence that will lead you into your make-believe tale.

Ebeneezer Sneezer opened his mouth wide and _____ _____

_____

_____

_____

_____

_____

_____

Today I learned _____

_____

_____

_____

_____

_____

Never, Ever, Pick Your Nose!

Remember: Bad habits should not be on display.

Pick a flower
Pick a rose
Pick a treat
Or pick your toes
    (Just kidding)

Pick some buttons
Pick some bows
Pick some jeans
Or fancy clothes

Pick some friends
Or pick some foes
But never, ever,
PICK YOUR NOSE!

YECH!

G.B. Lipson

Use your nose to smell a rose!

Here is Etta Kett. Can you find her hiding on this page?

Never, Ever, Pick Your Nose!
Student Activities

- Your nose is an organ through which you breathe and smell. Air enters through two nostrils where many complicated parts move dust, bacteria and fluids into the throat. Putting your fingers into your nose is not only unpleasant for others to see, but there is another important reason not to do it–it can cause infections and be very dangerous! Collect some facts about noses. Make a book in the shape of a nose and give it a title. Include information about smells, the sense of taste, nosebleeds, proper care and anything else you consider interesting or strange.

- Ask your school librarian for Shel Silverstein's book *Where the Sidewalk Ends*, (Harper & Row, NY, 1974). On page 75 you will find an unpleasant picture of a boy and a poem entitled "Warning." The first line tells you to be careful about something. Can you guess what it is before you look at the book?

- The word *nose* is a homophone. A homophone describes two words that have the same sound but are spelled differently and have different meanings. If I say, "The nose knows," that is an example of a homophone. Can you think of any others?

  - The <u>horse</u> is <u>hoarse</u>.
  - The <u>bear</u> is <u>bare</u>.
  - I <u>read</u> a <u>red</u> book.
  - The purple <u>flower</u> fell into the white <u>flour</u>.

- Imagine that you saw a little boy with his finger in his nose, and you said to him, "Take your finger out of your nose, kid. It's bad manners to do that." He looks right at you and says, "It's okay, because my big brother does it all the time!" What would you say?

Never, Ever, Pick Your Nose!

Writing Activities

Name: _____

Write a short story about the *dangers* of picking your nose.
Here is a starter sentence that will lead you into your make-believe tale.

Dr. Smelsey walked into the examination room, looked at Oscar's big red

swollen nose and said, " _____

_____

_____

_____

_____

_____

_____

Today I learned _____

_____

_____

_____

_____

_____

_____

20

Let's Hear You Say, "Hello!"

Remember: Arrive and leave with a friendly greeting.

Hello, Hello, Hello, Hello!
I'm glad to see you Jack and Joe
And Mary Beth and Sam and Moe
Hello, Hello, Hello!

Come in the house
And wear a smile
And greet us warmly.
Stay a while
Just call it out
In friendly style
Hello, Hello, Hello!

For young and old
We must admit
Hello is such a welcome word
The nicest greeting I have heard!
So goodness, gracious use it!

(And don't forget good-bye!)

G.B. Lipson

Hello!

Here is Etta Kett. Can you find her hiding on this page?

Let's Hear You Say, "Hello!"
Student Activities

- One of the cheeriest greetings that we hear, when we meet other people, is "Hello!" It says a lot of things but, most importantly, it is a way of recognizing other people in a warm and friendly way. Draw a picture of people in your neighborhood greeting each other in different situations. Above their heads draw balloons as they do in the comics. Fill in the dialogue balloons with different ways of saying, "Hello." (Example: Howdy; How ya doin'; What's up? Nice to see you; Lookin' good; etc.)

- You are in the shopping mall with your father. You and he are there to shop for new jeans when you stop at an ice-cream store. Your dad sees Chico, a kid from down your street, who is there with his folks. Your dad smiles at the kid and says, "Hi, there!" Chico smiles and says, "Nice to see you, Mr. Alvarez!" Your father is very impressed and says, "It would be nice if all kids had such great manners." With that incident in mind, make a poster that says, "Wanted, another courteous person like Chico." Reward posted by Room 232, Raleigh School. (Add your own positive ideas).

- Some words go together like *please* and *thank you* or *hello* and *good-bye*. What if there are visitors in your house and you have to courteously leave–what do you say to leave them? (Answer: "Good-bye," or "It was nice to see you" or "Thanks for the visit" or . . .).

- Hello! Good morning!
  The sky is blue
  The day is wonderful

  _____

  (Fill in the last line. The last word must rhyme with *blue*. How many lines can you make up?)

Let's Hear You Say, "Hello!"

Writing Activities

Name: _____

> Write a short story about saying "hello."
> Here is a starter sentence that will lead you into your make-believe tale.

Snobbish Sweeney wouldn't say "hello" until one day he met _____

_____

_____

_____

_____

_____

_____

Today I learned _____

_____

_____

_____

_____

_____

24

Respect People

Remember: All human beings and living things in nature are valuable.

Respect people of all ages:
Those who teach you honesty
Those who help you see farther
    and understand more
Those who are kind to others
And are honorable,
    gentle,
    loving,
    courageous,
    loyal and
    fair.

Honor the good people
In your life with respect
You are blessed by them.
They help direct your path
And guide your way.

G.B. Lipson

Respect one another

Here is ![Etta Kett] Etta Kett. Can you find her hiding on this page?

Respect People
Student Activities

- An acrostic is a series of lines in which the beginning letters form a message when read in sequence. Here are some examples of statements about respect which may express how the class feels about the meaning of this word. Make this whole class exercise easier than most acrostic forms. Use each beginning letter and put it into a word *anywhere* in your sentence. Underline the word in the sentence. Underline the word in the sentence on the chalkboard.

  R = **Respect** all living creatures.
  E = **Everybody** wants to be respected.
  S = **Some** people make you feel special.
  P = **Play** nicely and remember the rights of others.
  E = **Earn** respect by the way you act.
  C = **Courtesy** is a way of showing respect.
  T = **To** all creatures large and small, show your kindness.

- A *hero* is defined as "a respected person noted for courage and nobility." A hero may be a man or a woman who has many virtues. Write a short paragraph that opens like this: "My hero is . . ." Think about those you love in your family or special friends who may be your heroes.

- Bring a newspaper to school. Organize into small groups to look through the newspaper. Find the names of men, women or children whom you all agree are worthy of respect. Circle the article. When it is time for your group to report, give reasons why you admire the people your group selected.

- Imagine that you are a respected grandparent, who has lived long and had a lot of experience. What kind of advice would you give your grandchildren about important matters like safety, school or friendship?

Respect People

Write a short story about respecting people and all living things.
Here is a starter sentence that will lead you into your make-believe tale.

Lakisha pushed the old woman aside and ran to grab the last seat _____

_____

_____

_____

_____

_____

_____

Today I learned _____

_____

_____

_____

_____

Sticks and Stones

Remember: Both physical and verbal abuse are harmful.

Sticks and stones
May break my bones
But names will **always** hurt me

Oh yes they will
They always do
They get to me
They come from you!

They bite and sting
They give such pain
They twist and churn
They burn like flame.

If I were rubber
And you were glue,
They'd bounce off me
And stick to you!

G.B. Lipson

Sticks and Stones

Here is Etta Kett. Can you find her hiding on this page?

Sticks and Stones
Student Activities

- On construction paper draw a big bug to cut out. Make it good and ugly! Put lines on its back and write at the top, "It really bugs me when . . ." (kids whisper in front of me, start to giggle over a secret, stare really hard at me, etc.)

- There are many stories written about boys and girls who are picked on at school. Mean kids can turn on anyone at anytime and cause hurt feelings. Talk to your school librarian and ask her to recommend some stories to be read to the class that deal with problems like name calling and teasing. Look for the book *Blubber* by Judy Blume.

- The word *victim* describes someone who is a target for the cruelty of others. It can be anyone, large or small, child or adult. It can be any living creature harmed in some way by a bully or a group of people. To get a sense of what it means to be a victim, one may look at a sport called Riding to Hounds. This pastime, which originated in the English countryside in the early 1700s, was a fox hunt organized for the pleasure of hunters. A group of people on horseback would follow a pack of 30 to 40 hunting dogs trained to chase down and catch a single small fox that weighed 8 to 10 pounds. The red fox was chosen because of its cleverness in avoiding capture when it was threatened. This sport still exists today, and though the fox is frightened, he is not harmed. Write a short note to Mr. Victim Fox. Tell him how you feel about his desperate race to escape the dogs. Address the envelope to his den in the woods.*

*There are 160 hunting clubs in America today.

Sticks and Stones

Writing Activities

Name: _____

Write a short story about sticks and stones.
Here is a starter sentence that will lead you into your make-believe tale.

Nellie Nasty always loved to tease the life out of us until one day she came to

class with a very weird haircut _____

_____

_____

_____

_____

_____

_____

Today I learned _____

_____

_____

_____

_____

_____

_____

32

Telephone Manners

Remember: Courtesy is as important over the phone as it is in person.

The wires reach from here to there
The voices float on distant air.

How do they squeeze my voice inside
To travel sound waves far and wide?

Now here's a magic telephone
It takes my words into your home
It's like we're talking face-to-face
Though we are in a different place.

Speak up and keep it crystal clear
Don't ever chew your words, my dear.

Take a message!–Use a pencil!
Lucky that we're both prehensile*

Deliver the message from the caller
Don't give anyone a cause to holler!

I love you, Alexander Bell
Just how much,–I cannot tell!

G.B. Lipson

YAK!
YAK!
YAK!

*Prehensile: physically adapted for seizing, grasping or holding, especially by wrapping around an object.

Telephone Time

Here is Etta Kett. Can you find her hiding on this page?

Telephone Manners
Student Activities

- Telephone etiquette is very important. If you have been taught how to conduct yourself on the phone, then good for you! If you aren't sure, review some of the rules below. Ask for volunteer phoners to stand in front of the class and demonstrate good and bad manners on the phone. Don't lose your sense of humor!

Here Are Some Clues
- Make sure your voice is *alive* when you speak on the phone. Do not sound like a mush mouth! Do not sound like a robot or a toy that is running out of batteries!
- Always say, "Hello and good-bye" or "Talk to you later."

When You Make a Call
- Say, "Hello," then give your name. Then ask for the person you want to speak with.
- If that person is not there, leave a clear message with your name and phone number. Say you will call later, or just say, "Thank you or good-bye."
- If you get the wrong number, be courteous and say, "I'm sorry this is a wrong number."

When You Receive a Call
- Say, "Hello," and ask courteously, "Who is calling, please?" Don't holler into the phone when you call someone to the phone. Leave the phone and get the person quietly. Discuss with your parents how much information they want you to give out on the phone.
- Take a good message! It may be difficult for members of your family to return calls if your information is not complete. Always have a pencil and paper at the phone. Ask for the name of the caller. It is best to ask for the spelling because names can be tricky! Ask for the phone number and the message. Repeat the information to be accurate. Work with a class partner, and practice taking messages from one another. In class, design your own message notepads.

When You Call Information

- Have all the information ready which you must give the operator. Have a pencil and paper. Do the best you can with the spelling of the names of the people you want to call. Write down the information for future use.

- You may have noticed that some places of business may translate their phone numbers into a funny phrase so that they can be remembered more easily, for example: (289-6874) translates into "buy mush." Another example is 468-3647 which translates into "hot dogs." Your dial has groups of three letters assigned to each number.

  Like this:
  1. (use the number as is)   6. MNO
  2. ABC   7. PRS
  3. DEF   8. TUV
  4. GHI   9. WXY
  5. JKL

Study your own phone number. Work out words or a combination of words and sounds for fun, or to help your memory.

- 911 is the number you dial when you are in an emergency situation! We hope that you never have a need for this number, but you should keep it in mind. When you dial 911, the computer at that office picks up your address and phone number. They then know exactly where you are. The operator will ask you for details and the reason you are calling. Try to keep yourself under control so that you can respond. There have been many instances where very small children have been responsible for saving lives and rescuing people in trouble. Remember, calling that number is very serious business and is never to be used as a prank, because the call can be traced instantly!

TLC10014 Copyright © Teaching & Learning Company, Carthage, IL 62321

Telephone Manners

Writing Activities

Name: _____

> Write a short story about telephone manners.
> Here is a starter sentence that will lead you into your make-believe tale.

I picked up the phone and couldn't believe my ears. The voice said, "This is

Starship Rutabaga calling Herman." _____

_____

_____

_____

_____

_____

Today I learned _____

_____

_____

_____

_____

_____

How Do You Do?

Remember: Acknowledge everyone's presence and importance with a gracious introduction.

When royalty comes to tea
Make sure that you introduce me

The Prince of Wales will be dressed in tails
To him say, "How do you do."
His manners are great
From his shoes to his pate*
So ask nicely, "And how are you?"

Emperor Jones
In dulcet* tones–will speak
As he shakes your hand!

While the King of France
Will give you a chance
To serve some tasty tea

The gracious queen
Will brighten the scene,
And she'll smile to beat the band

So straighten your tie
Look them all in the eye
And the rest I leave up to you!

G.B. Lipson

*pate: the top of the head
*dulcet: pleasing to the ear

38

How do you do?

Here is ![Etta Kett icon] Etta Kett. Can you find her hiding on this page?

39

How Do You Do?
Student Activities

- First, a word about handshakes! Anytime you are introduced to someone, you may extend your hand to shake hands. If you are too shy with an adult, then don't do it. But, if someone extends a hand to you, it is courteous for you to respond with yours.

  The rule about handshakes is that your hand should be firm. No one wants to hold something that feels like a dead fish! The other thing to remember is that the shake should be brief. Don't keep pumping. It is also not the time for a crushing squeeze. Using these rules, stand and shake hands with two people near you.

- In front of the class, or in small groups, practice introducing your classmates to one another using first and last names. Then pretend someone is your father and introduce him to a person in class. Remember to use the older person's name first: "Dad, I want you to meet Danny Kipper." "Danny, this is my father, Mr. Gonzales." Do the same with someone pretending to be your mother. Let's hear, "How do you do?" "Glad to meet you" or "Pleased to meet you."

- Practice in a small group because it is time to make an introduction which also includes some information about the person. If you think about famous people, it will be easier to manage: "Mother, I'd like you to meet Elvis Presley. He's a famous singer with a terrific reputation!" (That introduction will give your mother a chance to be interested and respond with a friendly remark).

- Your host starts to introduce you and is so nervous she forgets your name. What do you do? (Answer: Introduce yourself graciously.)

40

How Do You Do?

Writing Activities

Name: _____

> Write a short story about introductions.
> Here is a starter sentence that will lead you into your make-believe tale.

The President shook my hand and she said, _____

_____

_____

_____

_____

_____

_____

Today I learned _____

_____

_____

_____

_____

_____

_____

Table Manners

Remember: Good table manners make every meal a pleasure.

For Alexander
Sit nicely at your meal
And never throw your food!
To mess the floor and table
Is considered very rude!

For Rachel
Sometimes use your fingers
But never use your toes.
Put food into your mouth
But never up your nose!

For Joe Ed
Higgeldy, Piggeldy, Pop
Don't be a mealtime slop
Don't mess like a pig!
Use a napkin or bib.
Higgeldy, Piggeldy, Pop.

For Jelly Bean (Geraldine)
If you say "yech" and you say "poo"
No one will want to cook for you!
Please wipe your tears and dry your drool.–
Then dig right in and eat your gruel*–
Pretend you're eating a hot fudge puff.
'Cause nobody wants to take your guff!*

G.B. Lipson

YUCK!

*gruel: watery oatmeal

*guff: nonsense, baloney, insolent talk, back talk

Coloring Page

Table Manners

Here is Etta Kett. Can you find her hiding on this page?

Table Manners
Student Activities

- Even though everyone in your family is perfect (that's a joke), make some signs to remind everyone in your house to observe good table manners.
    - Wash your hands before a meal.
    - Pass food to the right.
    - Wait for everyone to be seated.
    - Place your napkin on your lap or under your chin.
    - Don't reach clear across the table. (Please pass the salsa!)
    - Only take a serving size of food which you know you can eat.
    - Never dip your own fork or spoon into the serving dishes.
    - If a burp escapes your lips, simply say, "Excuse me."
    - Do not cough or sneeze on the table. And "heaven forfend" never, ever blow your nose at the table. Leave and use a tissue.
    - Do not talk with a mouthful of food.
    - Do not eat off anyone else's plate.
    - Don't slurp your soup.
    - And please don't feed the animals.

   Add whatever rules you think are appropriate for your family.

- Suppose you are helping set the table with your dad. He shows you where everything goes. You put down the plate with the fork to the left of the plate. A napkin goes to the left of the fork. The knife is at the right of the plate with a teaspoon and a soup spoon. A glass for water is at the right above the knife. Draw a little picture of this arrangement as a guide for others.

- Sometimes when we are at a formal table we are not sure what utensil to use first. The rule is that we always start from the outside of the place setting. Use the flatware on the outside and work your way toward your plate. Another hint is to watch others who know what they are doing!

44

Table Manners

Writing Activities

Name: _____

> Write a short story about table manners.
> Here is a starter sentence that will lead you into your make-believe tale.

I warned Jasper not to talk with a mouthful of food but _____

_____

_____

_____

_____

_____

_____

Today I learned _____

_____

_____

_____

_____

_____

Avoid Gossip

Remember: It is bad manners to gossip!

Gossip hurts a lot of folks
      And that's not the worst it can **do.**

If gossips talk about others
You can be sure
      They'll talk about **you!**

He said, She said,
They said, We said,
I said, You said–
      Comes from **whom?**

So don't repeat it
When you don't know
      What's false or what is **true!**

G.B. Lipson

Coloring Page

Say something nice–don't gossip!

Here is ![cat face](Etta Kett icon) Etta Kett. Can you find her hiding on this page?

Avoid Gossip
Student Activities

- There is a way to help you understand just how gossip works and how a story changes as it moves from one person to another–from mouth-to-mouth. We'll call it the Gossip Game. The teacher will start by whispering one sentence into someone's ear: "Stacey will give away free dogs." Then, one by one, it will be whispered to everyone in the room. The rule is that if someone doesn't think they heard the message, they must say the sentence out loud. Did it change or remain the same? You may use any sentence you choose.

- Humphrey Hateful writes a gossip column for the *Daily Blabber*. He writes about fine people in fairy tales, but his gossip is astonishing for example: Cinderella was a lazy, messy girl who wouldn't do a lick of work in the house and spread lies about her sweet stepmother and sisters. Goldilocks was really a short grown-up who wore a blonde wig over her black hair and broke into houses to steal things! Just for fun, can you write a gossip column about someone in a Mother Goose rhyme or a fairy tale?

- If someone tells a story about you that is not true, what difference does it make? (Answer: • People may believe it. • It travels far and wide. •It can damage your reputation and make you sound like a terrible person. • You can't defend yourself. • Lies are poisonous.)

- Make up a wise saying about gossip and hateful stories which can be illustrated and hung on the wall for people to read. These signs can act as a reminder to those who may be tempted to gossip. For example: "Loose Lips Make Trouble," "Give No Faith to Gossip" or "Never Betray a Secret."

48

Avoid Gossip

Writing Activities

Name: _____

Write a short story about gossip.
Here is a starter sentence that will lead you into your make-believe tale.

Motor Mouth loved to gossip, until one day _____

_____

_____

_____

_____

_____

_____

Today I learned _____

_____

_____

_____

_____

_____

_____

Tact or Diplomacy

Remember: There is more than one way to say something in order to be kind!

If you care about the feelings of others
There are countless ways
To protect them.

If you are wise, you know full well
There are many ways
To soften diffcult words you must speak.

If you remember a time
        when someone hurt you
You know the way
To avoid hurting others.

If you *want* kindness
Then *give* kindness
In words and deeds.

It is easy,
        if you practice.

G.B. Lipson

50

Coloring Page

Caring About the Feelings
of Others

Here is  Etta Kett. Can you find her hiding on this page?

Tact or Diplomacy
Student Activities

- If you are a person who has tact or is diplomatic, it means that you have the ability to appreciate a delicate situation and say something appropriate to make things less painful or embarrassing. Can you remember a time when you observed someone doing that very thing? Here are two conversations that were overheard. Carlotta saved the day in the first example, and Jake used tact in the second example.

Emilio: Look at that dog. He's the ugliest mutt I ever saw!"
Neighbor: That's my dog you're talking about!"
Carlotta: Hey, I'll bet he's the most lovable pet anybody ever had!"

Kip: Is it true you couldn't get on the swim team, again?
Susie: Just couldn't make it. I guess I wasn't good enough.
Jake: If I were as good a swimmer as you, Susie, I'd feel very proud!

- Was there ever a time when some kind person said or did just the right thing to help you when your feelings were badly hurt? Write a paragraph explaining what happened.

- You may have met people who are very sensitive about their own feelings, but they are not conscious of other people's feelings. Sometimes a classmate may say something which hurts very much, and they are not even aware that the remark was hurtful. Draw a picture of a person with arrows going through her body. Underneath write *Be Diplomatic, Use Tact* or *Be Kind to Others*.

Tact or Diplomacy

Writing Activities

Name: _____

> Write a short story about using tact or diplomacy.
> Here is a starter sentence that will lead you into your make-believe tale.

The neighbor's baby in the buggy looked like a little prune, but my tactful

Uncle Carlos said, " _____

_____

_____

_____

_____

_____

Today I learned _____

_____

_____

_____

_____

_____

I'm Sorry

*Remember: It takes courage to apologize,
but it's like a soothing balm.*

Just two words!
Two little words!
Two little weensy words!
A couple of itsy bitsy words!

So what's the big problem?
Why are those words sticking in my throat?

I'll tell you what the problem is:
I'm ashamed and embarrassed and it's hard
for me to admit that I said or did such a very
dumb thing and I hurt your feelings and I really didn't mean to and I can't think of an
excuse and no matter what I try to say it comes
out wrong and you're not talking to me anymore
and I feel like a low down dirty dog. No, that's
wrong, too. I know you like dogs!

Okay. I've made up my mind. Are you ready?

I'm sorry!

I hope you will forgive me.

G.B. Lipson

I'm sorry!

Here is ![Etta Kett] Etta Kett. Can you find her hiding on this page?

55

I'm Sorry
Student Activities

- Here is an opportunity for you to design your very own apology.

Kiss and Make Up Coupon Book*

This Unusual but Important Free Coupon Is From

Name: _____

Date: _____

❏ This coupon entitles the bearer to get forgiveness for having done a dumb thing.
❏ This coupon entitles the bearer to get one understanding hug.
❏ This coupon entitles the bearer to get a handshake.
❏ This coupon entitles the bearer to restore the friendship between us.

Print and organize your own coupon book full of kindness and gentle feelings toward others, including a coupon of contrition* begging forgiveness. Offer a coupon to friends, relatives or any person of your choice. Spread understanding and goodwill, and if you are sincere and lucky, maybe it will get you out of trouble. (But wait a minute, is it possible that some things cannot be excused? I will leave that to you).

- Occasionally, very sad or unhappy things happen to people young and old. In those situations when we want to be sympathetic and show people that we are concerned about them, we see another very important use of the phrase, "I'm Sorry." When you say that to someone who is feeling grief, they understand completely. Nothing else is necessary. "I'm sorry," says it all.

*With thanks to Dr. Roslyn Barclay, Associate Director, Counseling Services, Eastern Michigan University

*contrition: remorse for wrongdoing

I'm Sorry

Writing Activities

Name: _____

> Write a short story about apologizing and saying, "I'm Sorry."
> Here is a starter sentence that will lead you into your make-believe tale.

My father grounded me so I wrote to the governor for a pardon, _____

_____

_____

_____

_____

_____

_____

Today I learned _____

_____

_____

_____

_____

_____

_____

Courtesy in Public Places

Remember: Each of us creates an environment for others.

Dear Family:
Let's go uptown
Where there's kids and action
We'll act really great
For your satisfaction!

We'll shop and walk
And have a ball
There's nothing like
The Uptown mall!

There are things to eat for every taste!
(Watch your manners–pick up your waste.)

Use good sense; don't run or shout!
(You're not a circus roustabout*!)

"Wear shirts and shoes, " is a sign to observe.
If you don't pay attention, you won't get served!
          (without them)

So mind your manners
Always be sensible
And never do anything reprehensible!*

G.B. Lipson

* circus roustabout: an unskilled worker in the circus
* reprehensible: an act that deserves blame

58

NOW SHOWING!
PLEASE AND THANK YOU

TICKETS

Being Courteous

Here is Etta Kett. Can you find her hiding on this page?

Courtesy in Public Places
Student Activities

• Discuss all the kinds of behavior you have seen in public places. Think about malls, supermarkets, movie theaters, libraries, etc. On butcher paper, draw a class mural of things that you believe people *should not do* in public places.

For example:
• Skating wildly on a skateboard in a crowded place
• Bringing a dog into a restaurant
• Holding a dripping ice-cream cone in a fine clothing store
• Walking into a pastry shop with dirty bare feet
• Playing a radio loud enough to burst eardrums
• Spitting on the floor
• Littering the floor with wrappers and paper products
• Staring at a person in a wheelchair
• Talking and laughing loudly
• Running around playing tag
• Rushing past people on an escalator
• Being disruptive in line

It would be helpful to consult your art teacher, because some of these pictures present a problem. For example: How will you illustrate loud talking, the noise from a radio or other activities which require motion? And action? Look at the comics in your daily paper for some ideas. How do cartoonists illustrate action and sounds?

Courtesy in Public Places

Writing Activities

Name: ______________________________

Write a short story about courtesy in public places.
Here is a starter sentence that will lead you into your make-believe tale.

Blockhead, the class clown, was riding up and down in the elevator of Turnip Towers and would not let anybody in until the doors opened and a ________

____

____

____

____

____

____

Today I learned ______________________________

____

____

____

____

____

____

____

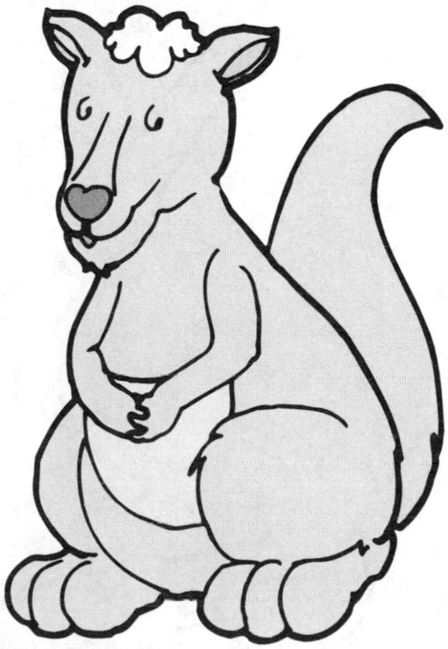

Make Friendly Conversation

Remember: It is mannerly to make conversation–a difficult but rewarding social skill.

DON'T JUST SIT THERE LIKE A BUMP ON A LOG.
OPEN YOUR MOUTH AND SAY SOMETHING!

What's new with your dog and how are you?
What are you reading and what do you do?
Do you like scary movies? Do you play baseball?
Are you double jointed? Do you visit the mall?
How was school on your very first day?
Did you see the good old home team play?
I have a wart on the tip of my thumb–
It means good luck where I come from!

Now it's your turn to think of things to say
and liven conversation in your
       own special way!

G.B. Lipson

Making Conversation

Here is Etta Kett. Can you find her hiding on this page?

Make Friendly Conversation
Student Activities

- This activity is called "Applause–Applause." Stand up in front of the class and tell about something good that you did this week! (Maybe you took out the garbage without being asked!) When you are through, the class will stand and applaud your efforts for having done something that pleased you. This is especially effective when the teacher has the first turn and tells about correcting papers on Friday night leaving the entire weekend free and unburdened!

- Think about a famous person you would like to be or choose an occupation you would enjoy when you are grown up. Prepare a name tag identifying yourself as a celebrity or a working person such as a musician, carpenter, doctor or lawyer. Pin your name tag on and choose one other interesting tagged person to talk to. Ask questions about that person's occupation and take some notes. You, in turn, will answer questions about your work! When you return to your desk, be prepared to introduce the class to your new acquaintance and tell something about that person.

- Find an interesting, funny or unusual story from the newspaper, a book, radio or TV which you would enjoy telling. Practice telling your story when you are alone, until you are comfortable and think you have it well rehearsed for your presentation. The class will break up into clusters of four students, and the stories will be told in those small groups. Each group may select one person as the best teller to present to the class. Set aside a special time in the week for these sessions. The stories should not exceed five minutes.

- Think about giving a demonstration speech to the class about how to do something you enjoy. For example: How to make a peanut butter and jelly sandwich, how to bait a fishing hook, how to do a dance step, how to use a bat, how to shine a pair of shoes or how to use a VCR.

Make Friendly Conversation

Writing Activities

Name: _____

Write a short story about friendly conversation.
Here is a starter sentence that will lead you into your make-believe tale.

I told my friends about an invention that would flip a 15-ton elephant on its side

so the zookeeper could trim its toenails, but they_____

_____

_____

_____

_____

_____

Today I learned _____

_____

_____

_____

_____

_____

Eating Out

Remember: All patrons in a restaurant are entitled to a quiet and enjoyable meal.

Hooray, hooray!
Today is the day
Round up the family
We know the way!

Choose the place
We're in the mood
It's the perfect time
For restaurant food.

The hungry crowd
Piles into the car
We're plenty hungry
But it's not very far.

Look on the menu–
what's your choice?
Let's hear it now
in a courteous voice.

Chicken and fish
to appetize!
Burgs and dogs
and golden fries!
Pizza, tacos, paradise!
Hot tamales to brighten your eyes!

Salad, ham and hot roast beef,
Yummy stuff to sink our teeth!
Macaroni, corn and peas
     Start moving away
          from the table, please!

Time for dessert–with fresh fruit pies! Eat it all and vaporize*!

G.B. Lipson
*vaporize: to be converted into a barely visible cloud of mist

Dining Out

Here is Etta Kett. Can you find her hiding on this page?

Eating Out
Student Activities

- You are in a restaurant with Cosmo, a school friend, who hasn't eaten out very often. A pleasant waitperson comes to take your orders. As she leaves, Cosmo shouts after her, "Hey, you, I changed my mind!" When our order arrives, Cosmo digs in like a savage. He slurps his soup, he talks with his mouth full and he is generally loud and uncouth. You are so embarrassed you wish you could hide under the table. Starting with "respect for wait-persons," what other things will you discuss with Cosmo? Make a class list on the chalkboard to help him improve his atrocious manners.

- Do you or don't you enjoy eating in restaurants? Explain. What was you *best* or *worst* restaurant experience? Draw a picture of a scene which captures any one of these experiences. Write a brief description below your picture. Do you have any suggestions for improvements in some family restaurants you have been to?

- You and your partner, Tex, have always dreamed of owning your own restaurant. You both love barbecued ribs and decide that will be your specialty. The decision is made to name the place The Boneyard, but Tex isn't sure. Brainstorm some ideas for a catchy name to attract customers, or you may choose to name other restaurants from A to Z. Some choices could be: **A**ngel's Pantry, **B**arney's Big Bagels, **C**harlie's Chili, **D**uke's Deli, **E**ats & Treats . . .

- Try to bring in a menu from a restaurant in your neighborhood. Design a menu based upon those you have seen. Don't forget the prices on the right side of the menu. Some kids order food without looking at the price! Do you think the cost of the dishes should matter to each individual? Why? Also design some terrific place mats that children would really enjoy.

Eating Out

Writing Activities

Name: _____

Write a short story about eating out.
Here is a starter sentence that will lead you into your make-believe tale.

I thought I saw a meatball rolling down the hall _____

_____

_____

_____

_____

_____

_____

Today I learned _____

_____

_____

_____

_____

69

Sibling Harmony

Remember: In a family we must be considerate of the needs of the group.

Oh, sissy poo
And brother, too
We make such harmony
Because we work together
A team we are, we three!

We never spit
We never hit
We share and share alike
For family peace and quiet
We never act in spite!

Respect, regard
It isn't hard
We make a happy team
We are so well adjusted
It makes our parents beam!

Good kids are we
A precious three
Can you be good like us?
Instead of hateful bratty kids
Who make a lot of fuss!

I know you feel that we're not
  real
By now you've heard enough
A threesome made in heaven
We're angels in the rough!

Respect, regard
It isn't hard
We make a happy team
We are so well adjusted
It makes our parents beam!

G.B. Lipson

Sibling Harmony

Here is Etta Kett. Can you find her hiding on this page?

Sibling Harmony
Student Activities

- Pretend that you and your family were going to have a serious meeting about getting along. Each of you fill out the following form to help in the discussion or add anything you wish.

I would like more

____	love	____	bathroom time
____	attention	____	allowance
____	privacy	____	responsibility
____	time	____	compliments
____	understanding	____	chances to express an opinion

- It is your job to write an advertisement for a baby-sitter for your sister or brother, and you must make it sound just right. Consider some good things about your brother or sister (everybody has good qualities)! Write an ad for the classified section of your daily paper that will get results.

- Are you an only child, an older child or a youngest child? Experts say that birth order affects your role in the family? Draw a picture of all of the kids in your family. Write a sentence underneath which tells how each of your roles is different. For example: Oldest child (has more responsibility), youngest child (is spoiled), middle child (everybody picks on this kid). How can you help each other? Read to the class *Tales of a Fourth Grade Nothing* by Judy Blume.

- The father of three children was getting tired of the daily arguing around the dinner table, and he found a good solution. Each child at the table was to explain one thing each had learned on that day. It worked very well in his household. How do you think it would work in yours? Can you make at least one suggestion for family peace?

Sibling Harmony

Writing Activities

Name: _____

> Write a short story about sibling harmony.
> Here is a starter sentence that will lead you into your make-believe tale.

Skippy was yelling, Mimi was crying, the dog was barking and I _____

_____

_____

_____

_____

_____

_____

Today I learned _____

_____

_____

_____

_____

_____

Anger

Remember: Talking over problems is a step toward a peaceful solution.

Listen up!
Anger can be dangerous

Learn to cool down
Take time out–
And wait
Before you make a move.

Don't say or do things
That can never be taken back
Or undone.

Walk away
Talk to someone
Listen
Compromise
Make peace
Solutions are better than
Fights and raw anger.

The peaceful way is better
    for kids
    for grown-ups
    for everyone
    everywhere.

G.B. Lipson

74

The Peaceful Way

1 . . . 2 . . . 3 . . . 4

Here is Etta Kett. Can you find her hiding on this page?

75

TLC10014 Copyright © Teaching & Learning Company, Carthage, IL 62321

Anger
Student Activities

- Establish a time-out place where individuals can go to cool down. When a person feels that he is calmer and collected, it is time to rejoin the group. What would help you most during a time-out session when you are upset and sitting alone?

- The Peace Education Foundation, Inc., publishes materials such as *Peacemaking Skills for Little Kids*. They suggest strategies which include sharing, listening, talking things over, apologizing and getting help. The idea of a "peace table" is also used for the resolution of a conflict between two parties. The rules are that: • Everyone is honest. • Everyone listens or speaks with no interruptions. • No name calling is permitted. •Ideas are suggested to solve the problem and be acted upon.*

- Perhaps writing about your anger helps to relieve you. Write a paragraph about something that made you really mad. Give it the title "Grrr" or "Blowup" or anything that captures your mood. Since it is very important that you also try to manage and control yourself, what would help you do that? What pushes your "mad buttons"? How could you avoid those situations?

- Collect socks, bags, yarn and whatever materials it takes to make some funny looking puppets to be used in a discussion. Add a touch of imagination, and give your puppet a mop of wild hair. Sit in a circle to discuss what makes you angry by letting your hopping-mad puppet speak for you. After describing many things that anger your classmates, discuss peaceable ways to deal with some of the problems.

Peacemaking Skills for Little Kids, Schmidt, Fran; Friedman, Alice, et al. 1993.
Creative Problem Solving for Kids, Schmidt, Fran; Friedman, Alice, et al. 1991.
Peace Works, Peace Education Foundation, Inc., P.O. Box 191153, Miami Beach, FL 33119

Anger

Writing Activities

Name: _____

Write a short story about anger.
Here is a starter sentence that will lead you into your make-believe tale.

Moose towered over little Sammy "The Genius" and shouted, "Don't call me

birdbrain again or . . . _____

_____

_____

_____

_____

_____

Today I learned _____

_____

_____

_____

_____

_____

Responsibility

Remember: You must answer for your own behavior; you are in charge of yourself.

I am bigger now
I am responsible* now
I am in charge of myself.

I have a job to do for myself,
For others
And for my place in the world.
I am responsible for:
The way I act, the things I say
   and what I do!

I will try to use good sense
I will take care of myself
I cannot blame others for what I do,
I will not lie–

Others can depend on
   me because
I am a responsible person
And best of all
I am in charge of myself!

G.B. Lipson

*Responsible: personal accountability; answerable for one's behavior; being a source or cause

78

I am responsible!

Here is Etta Kett. Can you find her hiding on this page?

Responsibility
Student Activities

Afterword
Dear Teacher,
The topic of responsibility was the hardest to deal with. It is the summing up of everything in this book–spoken and unspoken. The dilemma was: how does one, given the limits of abstract language, define *responsibility* and *accountability* without using those very words in the definition? This complex concept must be modeled by adults in increments, through every developmental chapter of a child's life. What is more–to develop responsibility, we must give children the chance to *be* responsible in different ways. This final lesson, therefore, is just the beginning.

• Here is a good example of learning to be responsible. Perhaps students have other stories to tell:

Alexander was quite young, and he was learning something important every day. One afternoon he and his dad lay down in Alex's bed to read a book together. As sometimes happens, his father fell asleep and left the little boy wide awake! Alexander decided to get up and play with his toys when all of a sudden he had an idea for a fun game. He started to pull his books off the shelves and make them fly in the air. He didn't stop until every single book was in a pile on the floor. Just as he finished this messy game his father woke up and looked around! He was shocked at the terrible jumble of books thrown helter skelter all over the room. He asked,
  "Alexander, what happened while I was sleeping?"
  Alex hesitated for a minute and said innocently,
  "A very bad boy came and threw all the books on the floor and then he ran away!"

If you were the father, in that messed up room, what kinds of things would you want Alexander to understand?
  • Don't blame other people for what happened.
  • Don't lie to escape the consequences.
  • Admit that you did something wrong.
  • Think before you do something.
  • Consider the outcome of what you do.
  • Please help to put the books back.

• What chores are you, as an individual, expected to do at home, at school, on your team or anywhere else where you may be accountable for certain tasks? What is your greatest responsibility? (Going to school and doing a good job for now and your future!)

Write a Story

Writing Activities   **Name:** _____

> Write a short story about responsibility.
> Here is a starter sentence that will lead you into your make-believe tale.

Rosita's puppy dog, Boodles, was home alone. He chewed up a shoe, tore up the newspaper and threw up on the rug. When her mother came home,

Rosita _____

_____

_____

_____

_____

_____

Today I learned _____

_____

_____

_____

_____

_____

Good Manners Award

We are proud to announce that

_____
student name

has earned the Distinguished Manners Certificate issued

_____   _____,   _____.
month   day   year

In Honor of Excellence, this document Is awarded in

_____   _____   _____
grade   room   school

_____   _____
city   state

OFFICIAL SEAL

I have good manners!

_____
teacher

_____
principal

82

Praise Page

My name is _____

I am a _____
(friend, teacher, neighbor)

I understand that the class is studying the importance of good manners. For that reason, I want to say something special in praise of

_____
name of student

_____

_____

_____

_____

_____

_____

_____

_____

_____

Ask Ms. Etta Kett

Have the students construct an authentic mailbox, as an art project for the classroom. The printing on the box will read *Ask Ms. Etta Kett*. Anyone who has a question or a problem regarding manners may write a signed note to Ms. Kett describing the problem. The writer's name will not be revealed.

The teacher will first review the notes to make sure they are appropriate and in good taste. Once a week the teacher will read a few of the most interesting notes in pursuit of answers, opinions and discussion from the class.

There should be a time limit for examination of each question, not to exceed five minutes. If a student takes only two minutes, he may choose someone for the remaining time, after which the discussion will be closed.

Example:

Dear Ms. Etta Kett,

   I was carrying a heavy load of books into the library, and my arms were full. A boy was going into the library, and I asked him if he would hold the door open for me. He said, "If girls want to be equal to boys, then hold the door open yourself."

   I was very angry and had to set the books down and make two trips into the library. I wanted to say something really smart, but I couldn't think of anything. What should I have said?

                      Sincerely,

....

                  Date_____

Dear Ms. Etta Kett,

_____

_____

_____

_____

_____

_____

84